History of Modern Masonry

A Look at the History of the Masonic Organization

Ian Day

DEDICATION

"Thanks to my wife and kids who put up with me. And to Abrandax Publishing for believing in my work."

Table of Contents

INTRODUCTION

This is an in-depth and fascinating look at the history of the Masonic Organization. On that traces the origins of Masonry back to the days of Moses.

Modern Masonry originated in London, England in the year 1717. It evolved from a brotherhood of artisan builders (or stonemasons) in the Middle Ages. Curiously, this was not even mentioned in the works of the early historians of the guild or in the first documents that refer to these groups.

According to scholars, many historical documents referring to Masonry were destroyed in 1720 by the founders of the Grand Lodge, for fear that their publications might produce negative consequences.

The intention of this work is to reveal the history of Masonry that has been obscured because its official founders did not want its secrets disclosed."

The Beginning of Masonry: London 1717

By almost universal agreement, modern Masonry is an institution of English origin, which started in London, England in the year 1717. On June 24th of that year, on the feast of St. John the Baptist (the date is important, because it coincides with the summer solstice at the time of the institution of the Julian calendar), four Masonic lodges in London united to form the Grand Lodge of England.

Six year later, in 1723, the Protestant pastor James Anderson wrote the constitution of the order (the constitution of the Free Masons, containing the history, charges, regulations, and so forth of the most ancient and right worshipful fraternity), which is still in force in its original form.

It is all too evident that Masonry did not begin on that date. The Grand Lodge of London simply brought together preexisting lodges, creating a coordinating organism capable of adopting other lodges under its own jurisdiction.

Several Masonic lodges existed at the time in various English towns and in Scotland and Ireland. The clearest historical proof that Masonry existed long before its official foundation and that it was widespread not only in England, but in all of Europe, is offered by the papal bull of condemnation issued by Pope Clement XII just twenty years later.

In it, he affirms that for a "long time" this society had been condemned in most countries as dangerous to the safety of the state. This is a clear reference to the guilds of nobles, which, in a sense, conflicted with the absolute authority of the princes. They sought to safeguard their autonomy and freedom of action, which must have been the object of repression in the most centralized monarchies and particularly in the state of the church.

This is not only about the structure, contents, and social rank of the noble guilds' members, but also for temporal reason: their existence is well documented during all the period from the end of the Crusades to the eve of the official institution of Masonry.

There is a substantial quantity of literature about Masonry that has not succeeded so far in throwing light on its origins. Quite the contrary: the deeper we delve into this literature, the more confused we become and the more we realize that it is impossible to arrive at any sensible conclusion based on historical documents.

All that happened before 1717 completely escapes any historical research carried out by traditional means. We know for certain that something existed before that date, but in three centuries of research, nobody has been able--or perhaps nobody has wanted--to find out what it was.

According to certain historians of the nineteenth century, many historical documents referring to Masonry were destroyed in 1720 by the founders of the Grand Lodge, for fear that their publication might produce negative effects. The first person who wrote an extensive report about its origins was the author of the constitution James Anderson.

Yet he limited himself to repeating what is said on the subject in the Cooke Manuscript, without troubling to give any information about what had happened in the three centuries that separate him from this document, and without bothering to lend a minimum of historical credibility to what it says about the origins of the organization. He traces Masonry all the way back to Adam.

The Apocalypse of Moses

For example, in the apocryphal text "The Apocalypse of Moses," the "treasure cavern" in which all the patriarchs were buried, undoubtedly refers to the same secret crypt of the Masonic Royal Arch's ritual, and the first patriarch, Adam, is a clear allusion to Moses.

If we take this text as one of the keys to interpreting Anderson's historiography, the origins of Masonry must go back to Moses, which is decidedly less improbable and wholly in line with the thesis outlined here.

On the same level, we find a host of works, mainly written by Freemasons, who claim extremely ancient origins, but in a vague and confused manner. What we know for certain is that the Masonis phenomenon was already ancient in 1390, the period to which dates the first historical document confirming its existence, the Regius Manuscript.

Of a slightly later date is the construction of Rosslyn Chapel, near Edinburgh, Scotland, whose sculptures recall Masonic rituals still in use today. These sculptures seem to confirm a close relationship between the Knights Templar and Masonry.

The intricate stone carvings are claimed by some to be a secret code understood only by the Templars and the Freemasons. When deciphered, the code supposedly identifies the location of the Holy Grail and the Templar's fortune.

Templar-Mason Connection

The Knights Templar began as Defenders of the Christian Faith. They were acclaimed and admired for their chivalrous deeds and good works on behalf of Christianity. The Templars safeguarded pilgrims on their way to the Holy Land and battled Islamic armies for control of Jerusalem.

The leader of the Knights Templar was Jacques de Molay, born around 1240 in Burgundy, born of a minor noble family, de Molay joined the Templars at the age of twenty-five and served valiantly in Jerusalem before being elected their Grand Master at the age of fifty-five.

Molay helped the Knights to become bankers of medieval Europe, and they eventually succumbed to the power of a greedy king and a complicit pope. In 1307, the French King, Philippe le Bel, accused de Molay of bribing Pope Clement V and had him and other high-ranking Templars arrested. In a tribunal in the year 1313, Molay was convicted of bribery and other crimes and sentenced to death.

Molay died what is considered to be a martyr's death and helped to elevate the organization's tarnished reputation.

In recognition of de Molay's leadership and martyrdom, the International Order of de Molay was founded as a fraternal organization for young men aged 13 to 21. Operating under the direction of Masonic advisers, it is essentially a recruiting service for the parent organization.

Masonic records trace the Templar-Mason connection back to an oration delivered in 1737 in the Grand Lodge of France by a Mason named Chevalier Ramsay. Ramsay claimed Freemasonry dated from "the close association of the order with the Knights of St. John in Jerusalem" during the Crusades, and that the "old lodges of Scotland" preserved the genuine Masonry abandoned by the English. From this historical connection spun-off the Scottish Rite or, as the Masonic constitution identifies it, the Antiquus Scoticus Ritus Acceptus, the Ancient and Accepted Scottish Rite.

During the mid-eighteenth-century emigration by Scottish and Irish Masons to the Bordeaux region of France, where they were identified as the Ecossais. The Ecossais extended the original three degrees of Masonry first to seven degrees and later to twenty-five degrees, and then evolved into thirty-three degrees. Mason who chose to advance beyond the basic three degrees join the Scottish Rite.

There are some claims that the highest level with Freemasonry is the 360-degree level, or Zero degree, also called the letter O degree, or O degree, representing the circle, hence the 360 degrees. This highest level is reserved for the rare few Novus Ordo Masons. Most of whom are or have been a United States President, British Prime Minister or other world leader or world influencer.

Masonic Lodges Before 1717

The existence of Masonic lodges on the European continent is also documented long before the year 1717--and these are lodges that were formed independently of the English ones.

Kilwinning is one of the first true Masonic Scottish lodges, and its existence is confirmed by 1314 (four centuries before the Grand Lodge of London founded), when the Scottish king Robert Bruce is said to have admitted the Templar exiles who escaped the persecution of Phillip the Handsome.

Even more ancient is the origin of the first Masonic lodge in York, which, according to the tradition mentioned in the Halliwell Manuscript, is said to have been founded n 926 by King Athelstan.

The Dutch lodge of The Hague called Het Vreedendall, for example, is supposed to have been founded in 1519. Destroyed in 16001 and rebuilt in 1637, it preserved among its documents the Charter of Cologne, the declared 1535 record of the meeting of the "elect masters" of the lodges founded in the cites of London, Edinburgh, Vienna, Amsterdam, Paris, Lyon, Frankfurt, Hamburg, Antwerp, Rotterdam, Madrid, Venice, Ghent, Konigsberg, Brussels, Gdansk, Middleburg, Bremen, and Cologne.

A congress of "stonemasons" was held at Regensburg in 1459, where nineteen "masters" from Swabia, Franconia, Bavaria, Upper Rhine, Switzerland, and Austria took part. (There are some scholars who see this congress in 1459, as the real birthdate of Freemasonry.) A few years later, in 1464, an analogous congress was held in Speyer.

The theory that receives the most support today among orthodox scholars of Masonry, and which is also shared by the vast majority of members, is that Masonry originated from organizations of artisan builders (or stonemasons) in the Middle Ages.

The hypothesis was subsequently developed and studied by various authors, especially Masons, who trace the organization back as far as alleged confraternities of builders of republican Rome or even earlier. Yet there is no documented or historical testimony that makes it possible to establish a direct link between the corporations of medieval builders and modern Masonry.

Freemasons

The most significant elements of proof for this theory are offered by certain building-related elements included in the vast symbolism of the order and the name of its members: Freemasons. Yet for an organization that was born in secrecy and that has a particular tendency to use substitute words to mask the real meaning of various terms, the public use of this name is not that significant.

It is not doubtful that mason refers to builder--this meaning is declared in all the documents, writings, and rituals of the Freemasons. The problem is that this is the name by which the members designate themselves, above all with respect to the secular world. The tendency of this organization to play with words, to encode them or disguise them, however ingenuously or transparently, is well known.

It is likely that the word mason was deliberately selected by members to express their decent from Moses, but that this was hidden under a different meaning chosen in view of the assonance of the name and the building connections present in the symbolism of the Masonic order.

The building-related symbols used in the Masonic order have purely allegorical meaning and are outnumbered by a mass of symbols and traditions that refer directly to Mithraic symbolism and to the traditions of the priestly family.

The building-related elements are the square and the compass (normally superimposed on one another to form a Star of David) and several references linked to the working of the stone. This is perfectly natural, for the priestly organization revolved around the construction of the first and second Temples in Jerusalem.

Moreover, at the time of the reconstruction of the Temple, Herod the Great instituted a special body of mason-priests, who were the only ones authorized to go into the Holiest of Holy for the performance of work inside there.

This body of mason-priests continued to operate for the following duration of the temple, charged with carrying out periodic maintenance. It is natural, therefore, if Masonry derives from the priestly family of Jerusalem, that it should preserve the building elements in its symbolism and traditions.

On the basis of the historical reconstruction, a large percentage of the European population has priestly origins. The great majority of European noble families, both of the upper and lower nobility with all their secondary branches, must have descended more or less directly from the group of Jewish priests who came to Rome in the entourage of Titus.

The question we might ask is this: How did this information come to be lost by almost all of them?

Josephus Flavius was aware of and proud of his origins, and the same may be said of the other priests who followed him to Rome. Even today, after over two thousand years, the Cohanim, who are descendants of the group of priests who became Christians and conquered the Roman world.

As far as we know, they seem to have completely lost this information about their origins. This requires a credible justification. It is, after all, the kind of information that ought to be unforgettable within a family--and the kind that would be impossible to keep secret if it were known to all the members and descendants of the family.

As the number of priestly families grew and the "organization" expanded, access to the higher levels had to be limited. One of the requirements for the maintenance of any secret is that the number of those allowed to share it must be as small as possible. Thus, the higher operative level had to be limited; knowledge was reserved to heads of families, firstborn sons, and those members of the priestly family who proved to be particularly active and gifted.

These were the only ones who knew the family secrets. All the others must have been unaware even of the fact that they belonged to a priestly line. Undoubtedly, they were aware that they belonged to the aristocratic class and possessed exclusive privileges, though they did not know the reason why.

There is at least one secret, however, which has not been handed down, even among the Cohanim: the secret of their Mosaic origin. Without exception, they all follow the genealogy officially established by Ezra: therefore, the secret of Mosaic origin must have been handed down exclusively within the secret initiatory organization, from which the Cohanim were excluded after the triumph of Christianity.

If this hypothesis is correct that the term mason, coined in the Middle-Ages to indicate people of priestly origin is only a cryptic way to indicate the sons of Moses, then in that period there were still initiatory associations that maintained the secrets of the higher levels. We can exclude the fact that at the time of the Carolingians, secret initiatory societies existed that were beyond the control of the civil or religious hierarchies.

All the great nobility and the bishops belonged to the higher Masonic levels--the one that, according to the Regius Manuscript, was convened by the king annually to discuss the affairs of the kingdom. Below this assembly of magnates there existed numerous local Masonic organizations of lower levels, and these operated under the supervision of the authorities.

Secret Knowledge

Some say that Moses was the first Mason. Therefore, the secrets of the priestly family must have been handed down only within the higher level of the initiatory organization. We are led to believe that all the members of the Roman senatorial class had knowledge of everything (all the senators of the fourth century held the highest degree of Pater) and at least all the heads of families of the great nobility, which had settled in Europe at the time of the Carolingians, who came directly from that class. In addition, the ecclesiastical hierarchies must have known about these secrets. From analysis carried out by medievalist scholars, it seems that almost all of them belonged to the senatorial class.

The continual references and the restoration of uses and customs of the period of the kings of Judah, together with the use of names of Maccabean origin among the upper

Carolingian nobility, a clear indication that this nobility was aware of its Jewish priestly origins.

Yet, what about today? Is it possible that the Christian branch of the family has completely lost this information at all levels?

We can conclude that it is unlikely. Even today, there must be a nucleus that is aware of their priestly origins.

None of the Cohanim--the Jewish branch of the priestly family--has lost the notions of its origins. The Cohanims' ancestors must have been members of the same group of Romanized priests that started the ascent to imperial power. Obviously, the obligation to secrecy held for them too, but because the status of Rabbi passes from father to son, and a rabbi must necessarily be of priestly origin, this knowledge has been handed down uninterruptedly within rabbinic families, and evidently in the Jewish communities in which they operated.

The rituals of the priestly family must necessarily have been handed down within this generalized Masonic system, but the more delicate and important secrets must have been the prerogative of the higher levels.

For the most part, they were transmitted orally, and consequently, we may presume that this took place mainly in stable structures that were particularly suitable for maintaining traditions and rituals in a reserved manner.

In addition to bishops, abbots were members of the priestly elite, because they usually came from the great noble families. We should remember that the Carolingians and the families associated with them founded hundreds of monasteries all over the territory they controlled and where they disposed the goods of the church, which were a form of wealth collectively usufructed by the lay aristocracy for their supernumerary sons.

Starting from the sixth century, various monastic orders sprang up all over Europe, and these attracted the cream of the aristocracy. First among these orders was the Benedictine.

It is likely that in these religious structures, where the line between layperson and ecclesiastic was often somewhat indistinct, the secrets, traditions, and rituals of the primitive priestly organizations were handed down (just as it was in these structures that the text of classical antiquity were preserved).

As a result, we must presume that through them the more markedly secular and organizational elements of the original traditions were handed down, especially those concerning the genetic origin of the various noble groups, which was the main basis of their rights to supremacy.

Given the proximity and the close connection between the religious institutions and the nobility, these two traditional currents, while diversifying, likely never have diverged substantially. Furthermore, in the period of the Crusades, these two traditions must have been combined in military monastic orders. They were called the Sovereign Military Order of the Hospital of Saint John of Jerusalem, of Rhodes and Malta, they were simply known as the Hospitalliers, for example, were an offshoot of the Benedictine order and the Templars were of the Cistern obedience.

Both were composed of knights coming from the low- and medium-level European nobility who took monastic vows but were part of an organization of a secular and military nature. Both knightly orders held initiatory ceremonies and rituals of an esoteric nature, and these probably sprang from the union of the traditions of the founding monastic orders and those of guilds of nobles from which the knights came.

Overall, these traditions must have reproduced in some way the original traditions, even if, given the vagaries of oral transmission, there must have been significant variants between one knightly order to another. Traditions and rituals of the knightly orders were likely also transferred to the guilds of nobles that multiplied all over Europe starting from the thirteenth century, after the definitive loss of the Holy Land.

The crusades, with the blossoming of autonomous and sovereign knightly orders and the opposition between the empire and the papacy, had led to the end of the Masonic system monolithic ally controlled by the empire and the church.

The city corporations had opened the way to municipal liberties--above all in Italy--while in the territories controlled by the empire (Franconia, Swabia, and the Rhine basin) numerous societies of nobles had sprung up.

These were composed of an aristocracy, which, by playing one prince against another, succeeded in maintaining a certain degree of autonomy and freedom of action.

These societies were spontaneous, free associations of nobles who recognized each other as equals (despite differences in titles and material riches). Each possessed a statue that members swore to respect, and they had given themselves rules and rituals derived from those of the knightly orders of the Holy Land. The influence of the Teutonic Order on the guilds of nobles of northern Europe was particularly important.

After the fall of Acrid in 1291, the order had taken refuge in Prussia, where it had created its own autonomous kingdom. From, there, it organized regular expeditions against the pagan Baltic countries, and nobles from all over Europe took part in these.

The journey to Prussia had become a compulsory step in the training of the low- and medium-level nobility. One of the customary ways of honoring the best fighters was the "table of honor," a ritual banquet that took place at a round table, following the Arthurian model.

These journeys contributed decisively to the integration of the European aristocracy and the homogenization and fraternization of the guilds of the nobles in their various parts. As a result, in the course of the Hundred Years War between France and England, French and English nobles who had met in Prussia honored each other and saved each other's lives.

The guilds of nobles, more than city trade corporations, seem to be at the origin of what later became modern-day Masonry.

This is so not only with regard to the structure, contents, and social rank of the noble guilds' members, but also for a temporal reason: their existence is well documented during all the period from the end of the Crusades to the eve of the official institution of Masonry.

Even if there were no such official confirming documents, we are led to consider it practically certain that these guilds of nobles were organized into levels of degrees, like the Carolingian Masonry and our modern-day Masonry. We know for certain that the emperor and the great electors of Germany were members of these guilds, which often met under the presidency.

In their case, however, they must have been part of an exclusive level reserved only for the uppermost aristocracy of the empire and who met regularly in exclusive sanctuaries.

The most important and jealously guarded secrets--such as that of Mosaic priestly origin, must by now have been reserved only for this level. Among the general population of noble families of a lower level, an awareness of their priestly origin must have rapidly died out.

Operative and Speculative Masonry

There is no doubt that mason refers to builder, this meaning is declared in all the documents, writings, and rituals of the Freemasons. The problem is that this is the name by which the members designate themselves, above all with respect to the secular world.

The tendency of this organization is to play with words, to encode or disguise them, however ingeniously or transparently, is well known. It is likely that the word mason was deliberately chosen by members to express their decent from Moses, but that this was hidden under a different meaning selected in view of the assonance of the name and the building connections represent in the symbolism of the Masonic order.

Among the arguments that various scholars present to support the building origin of Masonry, one of the most important is the fact that modern Masonry defines itself as speculation in contrast with the original masonry, which tradition defines as operative. The following explanation of these terms is given by Masonry itself.

OPERATIVE MASONRY: was an organization whose members worked with stone, squaring it off into blocks that could be used for the construction of temples--that is, stonemasons and builders.

SPECULATIVE MASONRY: refers to the organization whose members work on the "stone of their own souls." This image is sincerely poetic, but it does not find any correspondence, because it is not possible to determine a period in which the organization was composed only of builders or the transition stage when they were replaced by members of nobility.

The classic example of operative masonry, which is quoted by Italian historians, is that of the Comacine Masters. Some historians indicate these masters as the true founders of Masonry.

Tradition has it that they were involved for centuries in the construction of the Romanesque churches of half of Europe and, subsequently, of the Gothic cathedrals. Because they were Masons, as indicated in the Regius Manuscript, descendants of the priestly family associated in defense of their interests, the term "master" by which they are defined indicates an origin that is far from menial.

Confirmation in this sense is provided by the coat of arms of the guild: a compass above a rose with five petals. The compass is the most classic of the Masonic symbols, and the rose with the five petals is a common priestly symbol, which often appears in Romanesque churches starting from the eighth and ninth centuries and is present in the coat of arms of some of the leading European noble families.

Yet we must question the hypothesis that the Comacine Masters were the originators of the Masonic institution. Analogous claims with the same kind of proof and arguments have been advanced for English and German guilds that define themselves as stonemasons.

Some historians also include among the ancestors of Freemasonry alleged brotherhood of stonemasons made-up of Cistern, Benedictine, and Oblate monks, who from the beginning were masters of the science of construction and the keepers of the art of building used for erecting the great medieval abbeys. All the builders had to be considered Freemasons, but certainly they were not the originators of Masonry.

In the Middle Ages, the big business that moved the economy was the construction of cathedrals. Many priestly symbols are to be found on them. This is perfectly natural, because, according to our analysis here, customers and financiers usually belonged to the priestly elite.

In addition, those responsible for the planning and execution of the work must have also belonged to this elite, because they came from the best educated class of society and possessed architectural knowledge and notions that are still capable of surprising us today.

However, the manpower to build the cathedrals was supplied by workers of the menial, illiterate class who had to carry out the most tiring and humble of jobs.

The term stonemasons, which is used at times to define the members of Masonic guilds, cannot be interpreted literally. (The Four Crowned Saints are also defined as stonemasons, even though they were centurions.) The people belonging to these organizations were never simple workers, as a certain kind of populist rhetoric tries to show. Rather, they always belonged to the noble class or to the high clergy or to the group of great personalities of the period.

For example, Emperor Maximillian took part in the congress of stonemasons held at Regensburg in 1459 and in the following one held at Speyer in 1464--not as an observer, but as a member of the lodge. He personally authenticated the brotherhood book in which the results of the decisions of the congress were recorded.

His workshop partner was the great artist Albrecht Durer, who carved in the wood of the arch of triumph the effigy of the emperor dressed as a master builder. It is said that Emperor Rudolph IV was also a member of the building yard of St. Stephen's Cathedral.

The Regius Manuscript mentions among the members of the lodge of York only "dukes, earls, barons, knights, squires, and the great Burgess's of that city."

King Athelstan proclaimed to the whole country, to all the Masons of art, to go to him immediately. He held an assembly of various lords, according to their status: dukes, earls, barons, knights, gentlemen, and leading citizens of that city; they were all there.

Among Masonry members, it mentions Charlemagne, King Athelstan (924), and his brother Prince Edwin. While these testimonies are considered to be legend by Masonic scholars, other such testimonies do have true historical value.

The signatories of the Charter of Cologne of 1535, for example, include the sovereign archbishop elector of the empire, Wied; a churchman from Antwerp, Van Noot; the philosopher Van Uttenhove; Jacobs Praepositus, a collaborator of Luther; a member of the noble Genoese Daria family; and Philip Melantone, a jurist, a politician, and philosopher who was a doctor at several German universities.

All these, according to present-day theories, belong to what should have been operative masonry, made up essentially of artisans and building workers. Yet there is no trace of this in any documents. All the historical evidence indicates that members of the Masonic brotherhoods were always exclusively members of the ecclesiastical world, the nobility--including sovereigns--and the cultural elite.

There is never the slightest mention of simple workers. Furthermore, it is inconceivable that kings, princes, ministers, bishops, and abbots--the ruling class of a society where social divisions were absolute--should have desired to sit side-by-side with real stonemasons and builders-- traditionally at the bottom of the social ladder--and call them brothers.

Historical evidence demonstrates that the members of so- called operative masonry all belonged to noble families and thus of priestly origin. In addition, the Mason who were members of the first Grand Lodge in London were all gentlemen, that is members of the noble class.

Anderson's constitution, however, declares explicitly and officially that the newborn institution was no longer "operative" but exclusively "speculative."

Evidently, the terms operative and speculative are not to be interpreted with their literal, dictionary meaning. This kind of literal interpretation rarely happens in Masonic terminology. It's beyond a doubt that these terms should indicate either two different moments, or two substantially different levels of the organization.

If we exclude the officially sponsored interpretation, only two possible hypotheses are left: the first suggested by the Masonic ritual regarding the construction of the "spiritual temple" in place of the material one destroyed by Titus.

The operative priests would have been those in service of the spiritual temple. This hypothesis is attractive but not at all convincing, because it looks rather strained for many reasons.

The second hypothesis refers to two different levels of Masonic organization, and it is the more plausible notion. We have seen that in the first three degrees, it was possible to affiliate people who were external to the priestly family, who were not introduced to the secrets of the family. These degrees, therefore, must have had a function that was purely formative, that is, not speculative.

The higher degrees, on the contrary, must have been reserved exclusively to confirmed descendants of the priestly family, and all the truly operative functions, the political decisions and the consequent adoption of actions that were reserved for them.

The first few degrees, therefore, must have made the speculative level of the organization, the level where members of any origin could be accepted, because they were not initiated into the true secrets of the organization.

The higher degrees made up the operative level, reserved for members by birthright who had access to the institution and who proceeded on its hierarchic scale on the basis of genetics requisites (a categorical imperative in the Jewish priestly world.) They were the only ones entitled to access the sacred knowledge of the family.

This distinction never ended, because there has always been a level at which all the decisions of a political nature were made--which was above a speculative level made up of those proton-Masonic organizations that the Regius Manuscript describes as subject to the supervision and control of civil and religious authorities.

The Grand Lodge in London was defined as speculative because it was composed of lodges of the first three levels (apprentice, companion, and master), into which the members were "accepted" independent of any considerations of their genetic character, and which could not make decisions on matters of religions and politics.

The Grand Lodge remained speculative even when higher levels were introduced, the various ritual bodies, mainly the Scottish Rite and the Rite of York. These levels had no genetic connotations and no operative tasks, and they have none today, always remaining subordinate to the Grand Lodge.

We do not know whether there exists today an operative Masonic level(s) reserved for the descendants of the priestly families, or for somebody else, where decisions of political nature are made, and actions are taken. If it exists, however, it certainly is not part of the regular Masonic system established in London in 1717.

Starting from this date, Masonry has remained essentially speculative. Membership in the family of priestly origins is not a requirement and is not even known to members of the modern institution. Furthermore, it surely isn't included among the secrets that are communicated to them during the various initiations.

It's equally certain that the institution is in no way in the service of interests of the priestly family or of its individual members, even if traditionally, at the top of the Grand Lodge in London, there has always been an English prince of royal blood who, on the basis of the possibilities presented here, is among the most eminent members of that family.

The fact remains, however, that initially, and for at least all the eighteenth century, the vast majority of Masonry affiliates were represented by churchmen and members of the nobility. In 1723, the grand master of the unified lodge in London was Duke Philip of Wharton, and the English nobility was present in large numbers in the lodges.

The same occurred in the Grand Lodge of York, set up in 1725 in competition with that of London: it was joined by several peers of England, including members of the royal family. The Grand Lodge of York, which claimed to have been founded in 926 by Prince Edwin, designated itself and its followers as Ancients, in opposition to the Moderns, as the members of the Grand Lodge of London were called.

One particularly active member was the duke of Atoll, who held the position of grand master. In 1813, when they eventually united, the two Grand Lodges were led by two members of the royal house: the duke of Kent for the Moderns (The Grand Lodge of London) and the duke of Sussex for the Ancients (a Grand Lodge that referred to the ancient Masonic Tradition of York). The duke of Sussex had succeeded his brother, the prince regent, later George

IV, in this position.

No less illustrious were the members of Masonry on the Continent, which appears in the official historical records immediately after the constitution of the Grand Lodge in London, as if it were a direct derivation even if its existence came from long before.

German and Austrian Masonry included among their members Emperor Franz I, the husband of Maria Theresa of Austria; King Frederick of Prussia; the prince-bishop Count Kaffeeklatsch of Wrocław; and a long list of names of the great nobility and middle Eastern senior clergy.

Modern-day Masonry, therefore, was initially an institution composed almost totally of members of the aristocracy in the wake of the tradition described by the Regius Manuscript. After the French Revolution, the noble component was progressively diluted by access of members of the middle class, and today, no limitations of a social nature exist.

The structure of the organization and its rituals, however, are practically the same as those of the Masonry of the eighteenth century and have now been frozen in time for over two centuries.

Modern Masonry is no longer an institution that is reserved for or controlled by the priestly family, but this does not exclude the existence of a direct, continuous link between it and the organization created in Jerusalem by Ezra and recreated in Rome by Josephus Flavius.

The initial hypothesis that it reproduces the organizational structure of Sol Invictus Mithra, as a fossil reproduces the forms of a living being, appears to be legitimate and allows us to obtain reliable information about the original organization and its evolution.

We can therefore legitimately and confidently affirm that Masonry presents the underlying theme of the history of the Jewish priestly family from the time of its origins, and it allows us to look at even the family's most intimate and private affairs.

It's a story with many shady areas, and these gradually become more blurred as we draw closer to the present-day--but for the period before the eighteenth century, this history offers a sufficiently clear, consistent, and complete view to appear reliable, at least in its essential outlines.

Masonry in the World Today

With regards to today, we have an adequate amount of detailed knowledge of the history of the various national organizations of Masonry and of individual Masons to realize that it's strictly intertwined with the history of the Western world.

At the popular level, in particular in the schoolbooks, there is a tendency to ignore completely the role played by Masonry in the formation of the modern-day Western society; but it is beyond doubt that most of the protagonists of the history of the West in the eighteenth and nineteenth centuries were Freemasons.

The founders of the English Royal Society, which pioneered the modern scientific revolution, were

Freemasons, as were the originators of the French Revolution, whose motto of "Freedom - Equality - Fraternity" has been universally adopted by Masonry.

Many of the members of the first American Congress were Freemasons, starting with George Washington and those who wrote the Constitution of the United States of America. Likewise, the protagonists of the Italian Risorgimento, from Mazzini to Garibaldi, were Freemasons. In all actuality, the creators of the democratic system were Freemasons.

It's true that this fact is purely coincidental: they were Freemasons because they belonged to a specific social class, but their actions were not determined by the Masonic institution, because it was, as it is now, lacking any operative functions.

In fact, the majority of their adversaries and opponents also belonged to the same institution. The members of the Masonic institution belonged to a social class that historically had always been characterized by contiguous internal struggles to conquer positions of supremacy.

These struggles have become more intense and radical in a

period of profound economic and social change such as the modern age and have caused the reemergence of fringes of the priestly family once secondary or marginalized. This latest developmental growth is due to the rapid increase of their economic power. The have not, however, denied their origins, and indeed, they have continued to apply their hallmark to their most important achievements.

Washington D.C., for example, is built in compliance with a plan that is clearly Masonic in its derivation; the gardens opposite the Royal Palace in Brussels have the layout of a Masonic Temple; the one dollar bill created by the Founding Fathers of the United States is full of Masonic Symbols; and on the flag of the United States, as on that of the European Union, there is a series of five-pointed stars.

These are the equivalents of the markings on medieval cathedrals, houses, cities, and nations of Europe--designs that did not refer to the creators of the works, but to their owners who had commissioned them and had them built, the members of the priestly family.

Even if there is no certainty on the subject, it's legitimate to presume that, at least at the beginning, there was a higher level in Masonry reserved for members of the priestly family.

There is one indication which seems to confirm this. The Grand Lodge of London has always declared that it does not know anything about the beginnings of Masonry before 1717, and it favors any explanation or possibilities, however nonsensical, that does not make any reference to the rituals, content, or elements that could connect it to the Jewish priestly family.

Specifically, the theory of stonemasons is basically dogma, regardless of the fact that it is manifestly unsupported and not backed up by any historical evidence.

This myth is accepted as undeniable truth by the majority of the modern-day Freemasonry historians, but it is far from being proved. For example, the French Mason Paul Donna, in his book Les Origins de la Franc-Connemara (Paris: Ed. Derby, 1991), starts by saying: "In order to search for the origins of Freemasonry, is it necessary first of all to recognize its original characteristics, those that we must find in the institutions for which it seems to have originated."

According to Donna, these institutions could only be corporations of builders. All the rest of his work is reduced to the search for traces of builders' organizations throughout history, taking for granted that they were predecessors of Freemasonry.

It seems to be more than justified that this Origin story is a deliberate attempt to lead people off the track. There appears to be a clear effort to distract attention from what seems to be the only explanation that is consistent with the contents of Masonry and to divert it, seemingly successfully, in another direction.

Masons themselves, at least the vast majority of its members, are unaware of the origin of their traditions and rituals. They limit themselves to repeating them, generation after generation, exactly as they have been handed down, without wondering where they came from, and who set them up and why.

They recognize that these traditions and rituals are wholly tied to the Jewish priestly reality and revolve around the Temples of Jerusalem, but they do not draw any conclusion from this fact, and they continue to endorse with conviction the fable that Masonry started from medieval builders' fraternities.

It is unlikely, however, that information, which is, after all, of secondary importance for members, should have been handed down for centuries which limited alterations in the rituals and traditions, and that the most essential and fundamental information for the priestly elite--information about their origins--should have been completely lost.

Someone must have continued to possess it. In effect, there is a widespread conviction that at the heart of Freemasonry there is an important secret. Given the continual and probably deliberate attempt to divert attention from the true origins of Masonry, we are led to believe that this is exactly what the secret is about--and that there is a level at the top of Freemasonry at which this secret is known.

Since the Grand Lodge of London was created in 1717, Masonry has been basically a speculative system of belief, actions, and philosophy, which no longer has the same genetic encoding, and is accessible to everyone up to the highest degrees in the organization.

A minimum of knowledge about its structure, its regulations, and its ways of operating leads us to believe that Masonry might represent an entity at the behest of, and service to, some incredibly powerful and invisible forces.

Clearly, it's a system of knowledge that is susceptible to having its ideas, concepts and variations adapted and transformed into a structure that is completely different from its original form.

In the three centuries of its history, there have been numerous examples of this. Not least of all is the highly secretive P2 Lodge (Propaganda Deux), a private Italian firm, which, under a dubious Masonic facade, with the mission of infiltrating international power elite groups and governments on behalf of single individuals and rogue syndicates.

Yet these aberrations have always been denied by the Masonic Establishment. Regarding the priestly family, modern-day Masonry seems to have become an innocuous charitable fraternity. It's obviously not wanting to be seen as an instrument of clandestine power.

When the present characteristics of this ancient institution were determined in 1717, Europe was governed by absolute monarchs surrounded by an omnipotent nobility and clergy, who for the most part had descended from the priestly family and held all the power and resources of the community. The world literally belonged to them.

Masonry, however, was mainly composed of members of the medium and lower nobility. The reason to fit them into an officially recognized organization, controlled from the top, could be only to prevent possible threats to the power of the upper levels of the aristocracy from the lower levels.

We should not forget that one of the most solemn and binding acts required, then as now, from those accepted into the brotherhood is the oath of faithfulness to the institution and the authorities of the initiate's nation.

Members of the aristocratic class had always been united in the defense of their privileges before the rest of the population but engaged in a permanent struggle among themselves to achieve supremacy.

The dynamics of history and the evolution of society are largely a product of these internal conflicts. Today, the power of the nobility as such has declined, like that of many other branches of the family, starting with the Gens Lava of Roman memory and continuing with the Carolingians, and so on.

The instruments and the means of exercising power have changed radically because of the revolutionary changes of the last few centuries. The industrial, scientific and information revolutions have radically affected the social and economic systems that had allowed aristocracy to prevail.

New forces have gained the upper hand, taking control of the economy and political power. Nothing, however, leads us to suppose that their origin is different. The Star of David, the pent alpha, and a countless series of priestly and Masonic symbols appear in the flags, the coats of arms, and logos of most international corporations and most of the Western world organizations. It's a discreet but unequivocal presence--and behind all this there still seems to be the priestly family.

To realize this, we need only to look at the list of the components of the groups that unite the powerful "magnates" all over the world and who seem to exercise a decisive influence over the decisions of Western national governments.

The grandees of the world meet nowadays to discuss the destiny of the world and its problems, just as the overlords of the kingdoms met at the time of Charlemagne to talk about the problems of Christianity and to propose solutions and policies to control or eliminate it. They met in broad daylight, for all to see, even if it was in a reserved manner.

Today some of these groups have infiltrated and used Freemasonry for the purpose of carrying out their hidden agendas. Non-governmental organizations (NGO), quasi-governmental agencies, as well as conglomerates, universities, think tanks, and research labs.

Specific names of some of these world prestigious and influential consortiums include Bilderberg Group, Trilateral Commission, Counsel on Foreign Relations, Novus Ordo, Aspen Group, Bohemian Grove Club, Skull and Bones, United Nations, International Monetary Fund, Sol Invictus, Club of Rome, National Security Council, NATO, The Illuminati, The Club of 300, as well as many others.

The membership of these clandestine power networks includes European Monarchs, financiers, business CEOs and leaders, politicians, political advisors, media and news executives, university presidents, deans, professors, and regents. At the local level Sheriffs, Police Chiefs, School Board Superintendents, etc.

The origin of the Freemasons is as simple and direct as

their name. In seventeenth-century England, craft organizations began forming as a means of concealing specialized knowledge of their trade from outsiders who might profit from it.

The craft guilds declared that they were setting quality standards among the craftsmen; they were less open about their goal of ensuring higher incomes for members by restricting the number of people qualified to join and thus elevating wages accordingly.

Among the most powerful craftsmen of their time were stonemasons, who possessed the tools and skills to build strong, straight walls. The proof of their talents is evident throughout Britain, where many stone structures remain as solid today as the day they were constructed over 400 years ago.

Mason skills were rated according to three levels: Apprentice, Fellowcraft, and Master Mason. Each level of skill elevated the mason to a higher rank of recognition, or degree, entitling him to earn appropriately higher wages. Secrecy became paramount among the masons, who chose their companions carefully and swore new initiates to silence about the techniques they had perfected over centuries.

To provide control over their members and ensure that the secrets remained hidden, masons were organized in small community-based lodges with each lodge electing a leader or master.

A historical link with romantic martyrs garnered as much status for organizations and individuals 300 years ago as it does today. Adding color to the fraternal basis of their organization, Freemasons began to claim lineage from the Knights Templar. The combination transferred an organization originally based on the practical concerns of tradesmen into a fraternal assembly of upper-class businessmen and professional.

Once their association with the Templars took hold, many enthusiastic Masons began to build an aura of mystique around their group. Like all mystiques, this one acquired a patina of authenticity with time.

Scottish Freemasons claimed that several of de Molay's most dedicated followers had escaped France and fled to Scotland following their leader's execution. A few went further, maintaining that de Molay himself had escaped execution and arrived in Scotland, where he fought with Robert Bruce at the Battle of Durham in 1346.

Some still claim that remnants of de Molay's group escaped to America 150 years ahead of Columbus.

Freemasons and the Illuminati

Launched in 1776 by Adam Weishaupt, a Bavarian Jesuit scholar described as "an unpractical bookworm without any necessary experience in the world," the Illuminati ("Enlightenment") was created as a secret society the true objectives of which would be revealed to its members only after they achieved a "priestly" degree of awareness and understanding.

One of Weishaupt's early strategies was to ally himself with the Freemasons, a move that initially proved successful. Within a few years the "Illuminated Freemasons" were active in several European countries.

Thanks to the Illuminati, people would be liberated from their prejudices and become both mature and moral, outgrowing the religious and political restrictions of church and state.

Those who managed to survive Weishaupt process of selection and preparation eventually learned they were cogs in a political and philosophical machine regulated by reason, an extreme extension of the founder's "reason over passion" Jesuit education.

Illuminati members were to observe everyone with whom they came into social contact, gathering information on and submitting sealed reports to their superiors. By this means, the Illuminati would control public opinions, restrict the power or princes, presidents and prime ministers, silence or eliminate subversives and reactionaries, and strike fear in the hearts of their enemies.

"In the bosom of the deepest darkness," wrote one of the movement's early critics, "a society has been formed, a society of new beings, who know one another though they have never seen one another, who understand one another without explanations, who serve another without friendships. From the Jesuit rule, this society adopts blind obedience; from the Mason takes the trials and the ceremonies; and from the Templars it obtains subterranean mysteries and great audacity." Without a doubt this is a force to be reckoned with.

Freemasons Killed George Washington

George Washington resigned from the Freemasons and intended to expose the group's more reprehensible actions to the world. Washington was outraged at the plans by the Masons to erect a monument in his name, in a form that the plotters called an obelisk, but the president considered it something quite different, referring to it as the Phallus of Baal.

In an effort to silence the Father of His Nation, on the day he died he was bled three times by Masonic doctors. Under the pretense of treating a throat and lung infection the doctors drained Washington of almost seven pints of blood. Keep in mind that bleeding was an accepted medical procedure in the eighteenth century.

The Freemasons had already agreed that this would happen on or before December 31, 1799, the last day of the eighteenth century. Washington died on December 14, 1799. Without consideration of Washington's objections, the phallic Washington Monument was built, reaching a height of 555 feet--coincidentally the number 5 is a symbol of death and 555 is the code number signifying assassination in the Luciferian religion.

United States Dollar Bill

On the back side of every U.S. dollar bill is the Great Seal of the United States, a symbol many believe confirms Freemasonry's dominance and control of the country. The seal's design includes an eye within a triangle floating above an apparently unfinished pyramid.

On the base of the pyramid are engraved Roman numerals for 1776 (MDCCLXXVI), and the design is framed by two Latin phrases: Annuit Coeptis (Providence Has Favored Our Undertakings) and Novus Ordo Seclorum (A New Order of the Ages).

And if you look very closely you can see a weaving spider. Weaving Spiders is a code word for developing business and social networks. "Weaving Spiders, Come Not Here," is a deceptive statement that suggests Business and Social Networking does not occur at Freemasonry meetings. Curiously, "Weaving Spiders, Come Not Here" is also the motto of the Bohemian Grove Club an exclusive and secretive group of powerful world leaders and influencers.

"Weaving Spiders, Come Not Here," is taken from a quote by the first fairy in Shakespeare's "A Midsummer Night's Dream", act 2, scene 2. It's a petition to protect the sleeping Tatiana from the tiny creatures that are common in England.

Washington DC Street Designs

Architect Pierre Charles L'Enfant was a Freemason who was asked to design the seat of federal government in Washington D.C. in 1791. Various sources have suggested L'Enfant was pressured by both George Washington and Thomas Jefferson to create a series of symbols representing Freemasons and showing its dominance over American politics forever.

Among the symbols impressed on Washington's street layout are the pentagram, the classic Mason pyramid, and a representation of the Satan himself, all of them declaring the woeful intentions of the Freemasons and their absolute power over the United States of America.

Rituals and Degrees

Masons chart their status by visible levels of degrees ranging from 1 to 33. Today, there are various Masonic rites, among which the most important are the Scottish Rite and that of York. All those that are officially recognized are similar in content.

As already mentioned, there are higher degrees reserved for the elite few. Not much is known about these higher degrees.

The 1st degree, conferring membership is granted after the initiate dresses in a particular fashion, submits to being blindfolded, and is led to a locked door. His knock on the door and its entry to him symbolizes his departure from the outside world and access to the Inner Sanctum of Freemasonry.

After answering questions about his ability to follow Masonic principles, and promising never to reveal the organization's secrets, the initiate experiences the point of a compass being pressed against his chest, and he is asked, "What do you desire?" With the ritualistic reply from the initiate, "More light," the blindfold is removed, and the applicant can see his fellow members for the first time.

The 2nd degree is influenced by the upper tiers of the Illuminati; including the usage of the invocation spoken in German: "Wer war der Thor, wer Weiser, wer Bettler oder Kaiser? Ob Arm, Ob Reich, in Tode gleich" (Who was the fool, who was the wiser man, beggar or emperor? Whether rich or poor, all are equal in death).

The 3rd degree in most Masonic ritual around the world is based on something called the Hiramic legend, with ceremonies involving the dramatized ritual death and resurrection of the obscure man from the Old Testament Hiram Abiff.

The rituals from the 1st to the 12th degree are set in Jerusalem at the time of King Solomon and relate to events that revolve around the building of the Temple, with their various hierarchies, functions, and tasks. The episodes of which they are protagonists are not always confirmed directly in the Bible, because they are important only for the priestly family, but they fit into the biblical narration without any contradiction, completing it in a consistent manner.

The ritual of the 13th degree, the Royal Arch, takes place in the audience hall of King Solomon, and is centered on the existence of a secret crypt where there are hidden treasures of the priestly family, including the Ark of the Covenant.

The ritual of the 14th degree recalls episodes that took place four centuries later, with the destruction of the Temple of Nebuchadnezzar, that deportation of the priests to Babylon, and the definitive loss of the crypt.

The ritual of the 15th degree takes us about seventy-five years further in time. Its performance is divided into three distinct phases: It begins in the palace of King Cyrus in Babylon, with the scene of the Persian monarch granting Zerubbabel permission to return to Jerusalem and giving him back the treasures of the Temple of Nebuchadnezzar.

This is followed by the scene of the crossing of the Jordan, where the priests coming back from exile are attacked and must fight strenuously in order to get across. The third scene takes place among the ruins of the Temple in Jerusalem, when the priests decided to rebuild it.

The story continues in the ritual of the 16th degree Prince of Jerusalem, which regards the construction of the second Temple.

The rituals of the 17th and 18 degrees return to the theme of the loss of the secret of the crypt. The ritual of the 19th degree again involves a step forward of more than four hundred years: it is connected with the destruction by the Romans of the Temple in Jerusalem, the one built by Herod the Great. The ritual of the 20th degree is the one that narrates the decisions of the surviving priests never again to build a material Temple, but instead to construct a Temple that is completely spiritual.

The rituals of the 21st and 22nd degrees develop themes taken from the book of Genesis: the tower of Babel and Noah and the construction of the ark. The rituals from the 23rd to 25th reenact three important episodes from the life of Moses. They are all clearly taken from the Pentateuch.

After the Mosaic interlude, the 26th degree again takes up the story of the priestly family, moving to times of Domitian; the story takes place in an underground room and shows how the priestly family succeeds in surviving during the persecution unleased by the emperor. In this ritual, the participants are Christians and are responsible for the destiny of the Church of Rome.

The rituals of the 27th through 31st degree take place one thousand years forward, to the history of the priestly family.

The ritual of the 32nd degree is a simple one, the pinning of the Croix de L'Or or Cross of Gold onto the lapel area of the now exulted brother of the guild. This top level is achieved by great accomplishments that are in service to the Freemason Organization and for overall service to humanity.

The 33rd degree is the pinnacle of the visible degrees and is usually reserved for Masons of high profile and many years of dedicated service to humanity that have selflessly given themselves to the goals and missions of maintaining the Masonic Brotherhoods global influence and power. For example, world leaders, military leaders, and religious leaders, etc., are most commonly chosen to become 33rd degree Mason. The rare few are bestowed this honor.

As mentioned before, there do exist some other "degrees" of Freemasonry that are reserved for the most anointed of individuals. These can only be held by one man at a time and until death of that individual. Then the degree status is passed on to another brother until their death and so on. Analogous to a political leader or religious leader like that of a Pope.

These Masonic ritual traditions, show that they are directly connected to the priestly family of Jerusalem, and they also show that this connection passes through the group of surviving priests who gathered around Josephus Flavius in Rome.

Critics of Freemasonry

The initiation ceremony that includes covering the candidate's eyes during the interrogation ritual originally involved placing a hood over his head. "Wink," an archaic term for "eye," was associated with this procedure; thus, initiates were said to be "hoodwinked." Over the years, the meaning of this term has changed to indicate trickery, deception, and misrepresentation. Their opponents use this example to claim that Freemasons present themselves as something that they are not.

The early success of Freemasons produced critics, who feared the collective power of so many Masons holding high political offices.

Among the most vociferous of Masonry critics has been the Catholic Church, launching levels of enmity and suspicion between Catholics and Masons almost from the beginning. As early as 1738, Pope Clement XII condemned Freemasonry, saying, "We command to the faithful to abstain from associating with those societies...in order to avoid excommunication, which will be the penalty imposed upon all those contravening this order." Obviously, the Church wasn't merely annoyed; it was outraged and perhaps, threatened.

A few years later Clement's successor, Benedict XIV, identified seven dangers Freemasonry posed to Catholic:

(a) The interconfessionalism (or interfaith) of Freemasons;

(b) their secrecy;

(c) their oath;

(d) their opposition to church and state;

(e) the interdiction pronounced against them in several states by the heads of such countries;

(f) their immorality;

(g) their Luciferain connections.

This is no mere academic or theological difference; for almost 375 years the Catholic Church has practically equated Masons as a congregation of Satans. Leo XII, in the late nineteenth century, described Masonic lodges as "Bottomless Abysses of Misery which have been dug by those conspiring Societies in which the Heresies and Sects have, it may be said, vomited as in a privy, everything they held in their insides of Sacrilege and Blasphemy." Obviously, Leo's concept of Christian charity had its limits.

This eighteenth-century acrimony is not diluted by the twenty-first century enlightenment, nor is it limited to traditional Catholic animosity. Dr. Rowan Williams, the Archbishop of Canterbury, condemned Masonry as incompatible with Christian due to its secrecy and "possibly Satanically inspired" beliefs.

An earlier statement by the United States Southern Baptist Convention accused Masons of conducting pagan rituals based on the occult, leading the 18 million-strong assembly to brand Masonry as "sacrilegious."

Masonic Temples Around the World

The Bååtska Palace, Stockholm. Stockholm does not immediately seem to be relevant to the study of the ORDER of the TEMPLE--as it should be correctly referred. However, the country is a good place to begin. It may come as a surprise that Sweden has the headquarters of the only serious institution in the world that claims direct historical and spiritual descent from the Knights Templar.

This is the Svenska Frimurare Orden (Swedish Order of Freemasons) under the patronage of High Protector, His Majesty King Carl XVI Gustaf, and operating from the Bååtska Palace on Blasieholmsgatan adjacent to Stockholm's Grand Hotel. Possibly the most magnificent Mason building in the world, the palace would not be recognized as such by most Masons, some of the most common symbols such as the square and compass are mostly missing.

The palace was built in 1666 and acquired and carefully reconstructed to Masonic specifications in 1874. It contains various lodge rooms, dining and ceremonial spaces, offices, subterranean vaults, and even a throne room--the King Room--Oscar Hall.

Austrian Masonic scholar Eugen Lenhoff called the Swedish Rite "a revival of the Christian mysticism of the Middle Ages cloaked in Masonic forms." Many bishops and clergy of the official state Church of Sweden were and are high-ranking Swedish Rite Freemasons.

As one Anglo-Saxon Freemason has described it, on his many visits to the lodges in Stockholm: "The Swedish lodge room is a mysterious place, lit only by massive candles, where figures appear from the shadows to deliver their charges, then fade away in the darkness. The symbols and rituals of a Swedish degree are somewhat more explicit than our own, reinforcing the other-worldly atmosphere and heightening the shared experience."

The rite involves an initiation system of eleven degrees, which are probably the only Masonic rituals not easily found on the Internet, in major libraries or from publishers, such is the discretion of the Swedish Grand Lodge.

Members wear aprons, sashes, and swords in some of the first seven degrees, though daggers are worn in the fourth and fifth degrees. Where possible, some of the degrees are conferred in specially constructed vaults, cellars, or sepulchral chambers, with coffins, skulls, bones, and similar symbols designed to impress certain "life lessons" on candidates to emphasize the idea of rebirth into a new spiritual life and fellowship within the Order.

By the eighth degree, the Masonic aprons are set aside and the initiate dons a Templar habit, takes a new adoptive name in the form of a Latin motto, is given a golden "Ring of Profession" to be worn ever afterwards on the middle finger on his right hand and has a coat of arms designed for him if he doesn't already have one, later to be painted on a shield and hung in one of the Order's buildings.

In this degree and the remaining ones, the Swedish Rite makes the astonishing claim that it is not merely doing this in honor on the Templars, but that the rite is the true, legal successor to the Templars through a secret line of succession from Jacques de Molay's nephew, the Count de

Beaujeu.

As this inner doctrine is revealed in full, initiates are told they are also the legal and spiritual heirs to a "shadow priesthood" and illumination that the Templar Knights discovered at the church of the Holy Sepulchre. This was a hidden tradition that was earlier transmitted by the pre-Christian sect of the Essenes from its origins with priest Melchizedek himself.

The Rite of Strict Observance with its foundation from Templar-Essene tradition is what formed the creation of the Swedish Rite, which in time spread to most of Scandinavia and to parts of Germany.

Much of it also got injected into another Masonic system still practiced in some countries: the Rectified Scottish Rite, also called the CBCS (Chevaliers Bienfaisants de la Cite Sainte) --with its own claims to hidden knowledge that Greek and Egyptian sages subscribe to a religious dogma identical to Christianity.

The Grand Orient of Italy, which for many years was based discreetly at the Palazzo Giustiniani, which is near the Pantheon in Rome, the entrance is at Via Giustiniani 5 and still feels like it's in a dark alley more than an actual thoroughfare.

In Paris at 16 Rue Cadet, sits the longtime headquarters of the even more overtly political Grand Orient of France. This is one of the largest Masonic organizations in Europe.

Unique among Masonic organizations, the Grand Orient has its members join left-wing street marches dressed in Masonic regalia and singing of the "International" known as the hymn that the Soviet Union chose as its national anthem in 1944.

The Grand Orient's Museum in France includes a framed photograph of the Chilean president Salvador Allende wearing his Masonic apron next to a photo of his arch nemesis General Augusto Pinochet.

In the British Isles and on the Continent, Masonic lodges became popular places for men of different classes, professionals, and political views to meet. London's traditional craft guilds have retained their importance as social, charitable, and municipal government bodies, right up to the present day. While others have been and still are hotbeds of radical thinking, others have embraced clerical members and even such noted reactionaries as Joseph de Maistre.

The Scottish Rite (Rite Ecossais), later famous in some countries for its anti-Catholic orientation, originated with Catholic, royalist, Jacobite Scottish exiles in France.

Objections to Freemasonry among churchmen and political leaders over the past three centuries have stemmed from the brotherhood's Deistic, Gnostic, and anti-religious tendencies and its use by some members as a vehicle for secret political activities and subversion.

Freemasonry has also been accused of being a starting point for people that are curious about the occult. Aleister Crowley, the most famous dark magicians of the twentieth century, incorporated what he regarded as Masonic concepts into his occultism

Eccentric British weirdo, civil servant, Freemason, and "hereditary witch" Gerald Gardner basically created the modern Wiccan cult from scratch in the mid-twentieth century, based partly on Masonic concepts.

A different kind of occultist are to be found entombed in Washington D.C., at the Scottish Rite Supreme Council's House of the Temple on 16th Street, Northwest--a grand building designed by note architect John Russell Pope, who is best known for creating the Jefferson Memorial. The remains are those of lawyer, Confederate General, enthusiastic Mason reformer, and prolific esotericist Albert Pike.

In Vienna, Austria you will find the official Masonic Museum of the Grand Lodge of Austria. One bizarre object on display is a piece of art from 1979, called Baumeister aller Welten (Architect of the Universe) by artist Rudolf Kedl.

In most Masonic lodges, God is normally referred to as the "Great Architect of the Universe," but this disturbing Austrian depiction of the Deity shows a massively muscular, three-faced being wearing Masonic regalia and crouching down in the style like that of the typical drawings of "Baphoment", an orb with a menacing skull is at its center. The traditional pillars, called Jachin and Boaz, on either side appear to be the best possible public relations vehicle for Freemasonry.

In the early 1900s, three of the largest and most prestigious

German Masonic lodges were the Three Skeletons in Breslau and the United Death's Head and Phoenix lodges in Königsberg (now Kaliningrad, Russia).

The Masonic Chapel in Pushkin, Russia, 15 miles (24km) south of St. Petersburg. Pushkin was formerly called Tsarkoe Selo (Royal Village) in imperial times, and it served as a summer residence of the czars. Freemasonry was once highly fashionable among Russian officers and intellectuals and even Tolstoy's War and Peace gives some snippets of dialogue to the Swedish Rite members then active in higher echelons of society.

By 1830, Freemasonry had become illegal in Russia, which it remained until the end of the Romanov Empire. The somewhat run-down, Gothic-style "Masonic" chapel is said to have a bronze statue of Christ gesturing in a Masonic greeting, and the third-floor inner sanctum is only accessible by a rope ladder, where clandestine lodge meetings were held.

According to an article published in a mainstream, large circulation Masonic magazine and later reprinted elsewhere, the chapel was the site of meetings that finalized the abolition of the monarchy and sealed the fate of the imperial family.

Russian Freemasonry has been reestablished since the fall of the Soviet Union, although, Eastern Orthodox churches still forbid membership "on pain of excommunication"--at least in principle, if not always in practice. Exiled Russian princes and nobility in New York City, including Prince Serge Obolenbsky, preferred to join Holland Lodge No. 8 in Manhattan, and some still belong. Exiled King George II of Greece became a master of his lodge in London.

Rosslyn Chapel, Midlothian, Scotland

Rosslyn Chapel in Scotland is situated on a small hill overlooking Roslin Glen, close to the village of Roslin, in Midlothian, six miles south of Edinburgh. It was founded in 1456 by William St. Clair, first Earl of Caithness, as the Collegiate Church of St. Matthew, one of the nearly forty such collegiate churches in Scotland before the Reformation and housed up to six canons (priests) and two boys' choristers.

Its purpose was to celebrate the Divine Office daily and to sing Masses for the repose of the souls of the dead, particularly deceased members of the St. Clair Family. There was a permanent endowment to support this establishment, which endured until the Reformation in Scotland (1560).

The provost was then driven out and the altars were smashed. In the seventeenth century, when Oliver Cromwell invaded Scotland, his troops used the chapel as a stable, but they left its many rich carvings largely intact. In 1861 it once again became a place of worship, this time under the aegis of the Scottish Episcopal Church, as it remains today.

Legend has it that William St. Clair, was a Knight Templar; that the building is a rich trove of Templar lore; that its stone carvings illustrate many of the Templar and Masonic secrets; and that its vault conceals a buried treasure of the Templars, the Holy Grail and even the head of Jesus Christ.

It is further maintained that the St. Clairs, in their seagoing adventures of Orkney, had discovered America before Columbus and that medieval carvings in the chapel illustrated a type of corn found only in the New World at that time.

Some of these claims are based on features of the building that are indeed spectacular. The chapel is supported by fourteen pillars that form twelve arches on three sides of the nave. The three pillars at the east end are now known as the Master Pillar, the Journeyman Pillar, and the Apprentice Pillar. The Apprentice Pillar is named after the stone master that was in charge of crafting and delegated the work to an apprentice who was better at carving than he was--this caused the jealous master to murder him.

The three pillars' original, medieval names were the Earl's Pillar (the chapel's founder being the Earl of Caithness), Shekinah (meaning "the presence of God," a traditional Christian usage from biblical sources and a natural attribution for the east end of a church were Mass was celebrated ad orientem), and the Prince's Pillar (the St. Clairs were also princes of Orkney), sometimes known as "Matthew's Staff," since it held up a chapel dedicated to St. Matthew.

Some propose that the notion of Shekinah derives originally from the Temple of Solomon at Jerusalem and that Rosslyn is modeled on the layout of the original Temple. However, the chapel was designed as a much larger, cruciform church, of which the existing building was intended to be only the choir and Lady Chapel.

A series of carvings in the chapel are a cradle to grave representation of life--more than 110 in all--of human heads surrounded by greenery. They depict the progression through life to death, moving from east to west (sunrise to sunset) in the chapel, the first carvings illustrating youth and spring, the final ones are reduced to skulls.

Final Thoughts

What is striking about Freemasonry is the apparent lack of homogeneity of the members. Yet when we analyze their names and their origins, we realize that what unite most of these people is their genetic make-up--that is, the majority of them belong to the stock of those family groups, which have been identified as descendants of the Mosaic priestly family. Today, yesterday, and tomorrow, the world still belongs to them.

"When in your house black crows sire white doves, then you shall be called wise."

-Motto of the Croix de L'or

93

ABOUT THE AUTHOR

Ian Day lives with his wife, two children, and three cats on his 35 acre ranch, Rancho Diablo, outside of Winslow, Arizona.

www.ingramcontent.com/pod-product-compliance
Lightning Source LLC
Chambersburg PA
CBHW070837260726
48660CB00005B/2074